Science Inquiry
WHAT DO
PLANTS NEED
TO SURVIVE?

by Emily Raij

T0050850

PEBBLE
a capstone imprint

Pebble Explore is published by Pebble, an imprint of Capstone.
1710 Roe Crest Drive
North Mankato, Minnesota 56003
www.capstonepub.com

Library of Congress Cataloging-in-Publication Data
Names: Raij, Emily, author.
Title: What do plants need to survive? / by Emily Raij.
Description: North Mankato, Minnesota : Pebble, [2022] | Series: Science inquiry | Includes bibliographical references and index. | Audience: Ages 5-8 | Audience: Grades 2-3 | Summary: "Plants are living things. They need certain things to grow and live. What are they? Let's investigate what plants need to survive!"— Provided by publisher.
Identifiers: LCCN 2021002753 (print) | LCCN 2021002754 (ebook) | ISBN 9781977131447 (hardcover) | ISBN 9781977132611 (paperback) | ISBN 9781977155290 (pdf) | ISBN 9781977156914 (kindle edition)
Subjects: LCSH: Plant physiology—Juvenile literature. | Plants—Juvenile literature. | Life (Biology)—Juvenile literature. | Plants—Habitat—Juvenile literature.
Classification: LCC QK711.5 .R35 2022 (print) | LCC QK711.5 (ebook) | DDC 581—dc23
LC record available at https://lccn.loc.gov/2021002753
LC ebook record available at https://lccn.loc.gov/202100275

Image Credits
Getty Images/FarCamera, 6; Shutterstock: Alex Lerner, 28, Anna Nahabed, 15, Belozorova Elena, cover, Dmitrydesign, 1, 22, Fotos593, 27, gstraub, 13, HDsert, 25, J. Photo, 20, Lidiane Miotto, 17, Lyu Hu, 29, Rawpixel.com, 7, 11, SantaLiza, 16, SariMe, 19, Schira, 9, Vasilyev Aleksandr, 23, Viktor Ronnert, 5

Artistic elements: Shutterstock/balabolka

Editorial Credits
Editor: Erika L. Shores; Designers: Dina Her and Juliette Peters; Media Researcher: Kelly Garvin; Production Specialist: Tori Abraham

All internet sites appearing in back matter were available and accurate when this book was sent to press.

TABLE OF CONTENTS

Words in **bold** are in the glossary.

A PLANT INVESTIGATION

Drooping leaves. Brown edges. Dry soil. Your plant is not looking good. But it looked great when you brought it home. Its leaves were green. The soil was moist. What happened?

Not everyone has a green thumb. People say you have a green thumb if you are good at growing things. But plants need more than that to live. They need water, sunlight, and air. **Shelter** and enough space help plants grow too. Are you ready to work on that green thumb?

Let's do an investigation to see for ourselves what plants need. Plant bean sprouts in six paper or plastic cups.

One is the **control** plant. It gets everything it needs. Place this plant on the windowsill. Water it every two days.

The control plant is getting sun, water, and good soil with **fertilizer**, or plant food. It has enough air. The room stays at a steady temperature. It doesn't get too hot or too cold.

The other plants are test plants. You will change the way you care for each plant. You will take away one of the things each plant needs.

Place a paper bag over one plant. Still give the plant water and good soil.

Place another plant in a freezer. This plant still gets good soil and water.

Put the third plant on a windowsill. Give it good soil but no water.

Put the fourth plant in a sealed plastic bag. No air can get in or out. This plant goes in a spot with some shade to not overheat. It gets water and good soil.

Place the fifth plant on the windowsill. The plant gets water but poor soil without fertilizer.

Check each of the plants every two days. Write down what you see.

When you check on the plants, water them unless that need was taken away. After two weeks, which plants look healthy? Which ones do not?

WHAT DO PLANTS NEED TO LIVE?

What did you find out? Plants need water, good soil, sunlight, air, and a steady temperature to live. Different plants need these things in different amounts. These needs help plants do a special job. That job is called **photosynthesis**.

Photosynthesis is the process plants use to make their own food. People get their food from plants or animals. Food is what gives living things energy. Almost all living things depend on photosynthesis to survive.

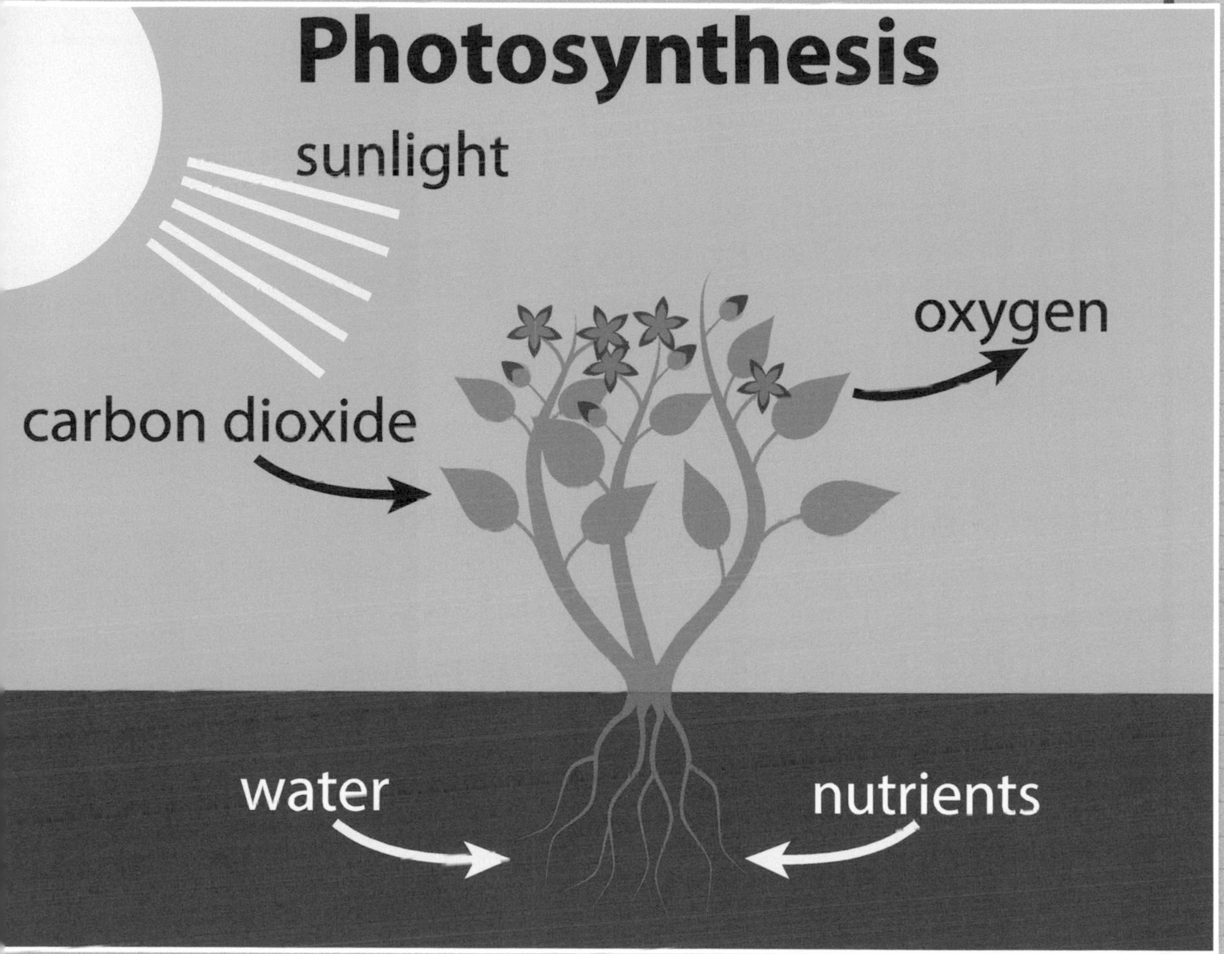

Photosynthesis

sunlight

oxygen

carbon dioxide

water

nutrients

Plants growing outside get the sun, rain, soil, and air they need. Indoor plants need people to help. We water them. We give them fertilizer. We place them in the sun or shade.

If plants don't look healthy, we can make changes. That might mean more water. Or maybe they need a little less sunlight. Let's dig deeper to see how plants get what they need to make food.

HOW DO PLANTS GET WATER AND NUTRIENTS?

Plants that grow outside get water from rain and dew. They also pull water from the air. Plant cells are mostly made up of water. It keeps plants strong and standing up. When you see a **wilted** plant, it probably needs a drink!

Water also moves **nutrients** through the plant. Plants get nutrients and water from soil. Plants **absorb** water and nutrients through their roots. Roots grow underground, where they can take in the most water and nutrients.

Think about your investigation. What happened to the plants that didn't get enough water or nutrients? They didn't look so good after two weeks. Some may have died.

The soil matters too. Soil that is too sandy might not hold enough water. Some soil is missing nutrients. Wind can blow good soil away. Rain can wash it away too.

HOW DO PLANTS GET SUNLIGHT AND AIR?

Now think about the plants from the investigation that didn't get enough air or sun. They didn't look healthy either. They didn't get what they needed to make food.

Plants breathe! They take in air through tiny holes in their leaves. They need plenty of clean air.

Plants also help clean our air. People breathe out **carbon dioxide**. Too much of that gas is unsafe for us to breathe in. But not plants! They use carbon dioxide, plus water and sunlight, to make their food. They also release **oxygen**. That is a good gas people need to breathe.

Have you noticed that many leaves are wide and flat? This shape lets them trap more sunlight. But too much heat can burn plants. Plants also lose water when it's too hot.

Some plants can survive cold weather. Others cannot. Too much cold can freeze plants. That is what happened to the freezer plants from the investigation.

Plants change with the seasons. Spring rain and summer sun bring more growth. Colder weather and shorter days in fall and winter mean less sun. Plants are **dormant** then. They don't grow.

WHY DO PLANTS NEED SPACE AND SHELTER?

Plants can live in many different places. There are forests full of trees. A porch garden can bloom with herbs. Other plants grow under oceans. Dandelions might peek out of a sidewalk crack.

Plants' **habitats** give them everything they need. But these spaces can get crowded. That causes plants to fight for nutrients, water, and sunlight. Some will get enough. Others won't.

Plants need space to grow. Roots need room to spread out underground. Leaves need space to stretch out. Tight spaces can cause plants to stay small and not get enough air.

Shelter is important too. Plants grow where they can stay safe from harsh weather. Some plants need more shade. They grow under taller plants that block the sun.

HOW DO PLANTS ADAPT?

Not all plants can live in hot, dry deserts. The ones that can have **adapted**. Consider the cactus. It doesn't need much water. It can survive strong sun. Its roots grow close to the surface. They soak up water before it dries up.

Plants adapt in other ways too. Plant seeds have hard coverings to protect them from cold. Some seeds can stick to animal fur. Others are shaped to be carried by the wind. This spreads seeds around to more places to grow. From their roots to their seeds, plants are made to survive.

GLOSSARY

absorb (ab-ZORB)—to soak up

adapt (uh-DAPT)—to change in order to survive

carbon dioxide (KAHR-buhn dy-AHK-syd)—a colorless, odorless gas that people and animals breathe out; plants take in carbon dioxide because they need it to live

control (kuhn-TROHL)—a group in an experiment that is not being treated

dormant (DOR-muhnt)—not active

fertilizer (FUHR-tuh-ly-zuhr)—a substance added to soil to make crops grow better

habitat (HAB-uh-tat)—the home of a plant or animal

nutrient (NOO-tree-uhnt)—something that is needed by people, animals, and plants to stay healthy and strong

oxygen (OK-suh-juhn)—a colorless gas that people and animals breathe; humans and animals need oxygen to live

photosynthesis (foh-toh-SIN-thuh-siss)—the process by which green plants make their food

shelter (SHEL-tur)—a safe, covered place

wilt (WILT)—to droop; some plants lose water and bend over in heat

READ MORE

Gaines, Joanna. *We Are the Gardeners*. Nashville, TN: Thomas Nelson, 2019.

Lindeen, Mary. *What Plants Need*. Fairport, NY: Norwood House Press, 2019.

Machajewski, Sarah. *How Plants Protect Themselves*. New York: Gareth Stevens Publishing, 2020.

INTERNET SITES

How Plants Grow
dkfindout.com/us/animals-and-nature/plants/how-plants-grow/

How Plants Grow Video for Kids
easyscienceforkids.com/how-plants-grow-video-for-kids/

Plant Facts for Kids
coolkidfacts.com/plant-facts-for-kids/

INDEX